NATIONAL GEOGRAPHIC

Ladders

Earth's Crazy Climate

GENRE Science Article

Read to find out about the last ice age.

When the Ice Melted

by Richard Easby illustrations by Bob Kayganich

Imagine that you take a time machine back to 18,000 years ago. When you arrive, a freezing wind pulls at your coat and numbs your face. The air is dry and filled with fine dust. As your eyes adjust to the hazy light, a barren scene comes into focus. All you can see is ice stretching to the horizon. You've landed on top of an **ice sheet**! Welcome to the last ice age.

At this time in Earth's past, about one-third of the planet is icebound. A few massive ice sheets cover present-day Canada and much of the northern United States. Northern Europe and northern Asia are also buried beneath ice sheets. Everywhere the ice is thick. For example, an ice sheet at least 1,220 meters (4,003 feet) thick covered mountains in present-day Vermont.

THE BIG CHILL Scientists have many theories as to what caused the big chill. Many say the shape of Earth's orbit changed slightly, causing less direct sunlight to reach the planet. This changed Earth's **climate.** Temperatures dropped, and snow and ice piled up, forming ice sheets. As the ice sheets grew larger, they chilled nearby lands, turning them into frozen deserts. Miles away, many animals lived in shallow valleys that were protected from the frigid winds. You may recognize some of these animals, but others were unusual.

WOOLLY AND WARM Woolly mammoths lived on the cold, flat, treeless **tundra.** They looked like elephants, but they were covered with hair that grew 1 meter (3 feet) long. Under the hair was a layer of warm wool, and beneath the skin was a layer of fat. The hair, wool, and fat kept these giant animals warm.

Ice Age humans lived in small groups in shallow river valleys. The climate was cold and dry. Fewer plants were available to eat. Humans hunted herds of woolly mammoths, antelope, and other large animals for food.

An Icier Earth

NATURE'S BULLDOZERS You may think nothing happened to Earth during this time. After all, a lot of land was buried under ice. Ice sheets, however, don't just sit there—they move! Ice sheets move slowly, sometimes only 3 centimeters (1 inch) per year. Ice sheets are extremely heavy, too. As they advanced, they shoveled and moved tons of rock and soil. These giant bulldozers of ice reshaped the land by shaving off mountaintops, widening valleys, and dumping huge amounts of rocky debris.

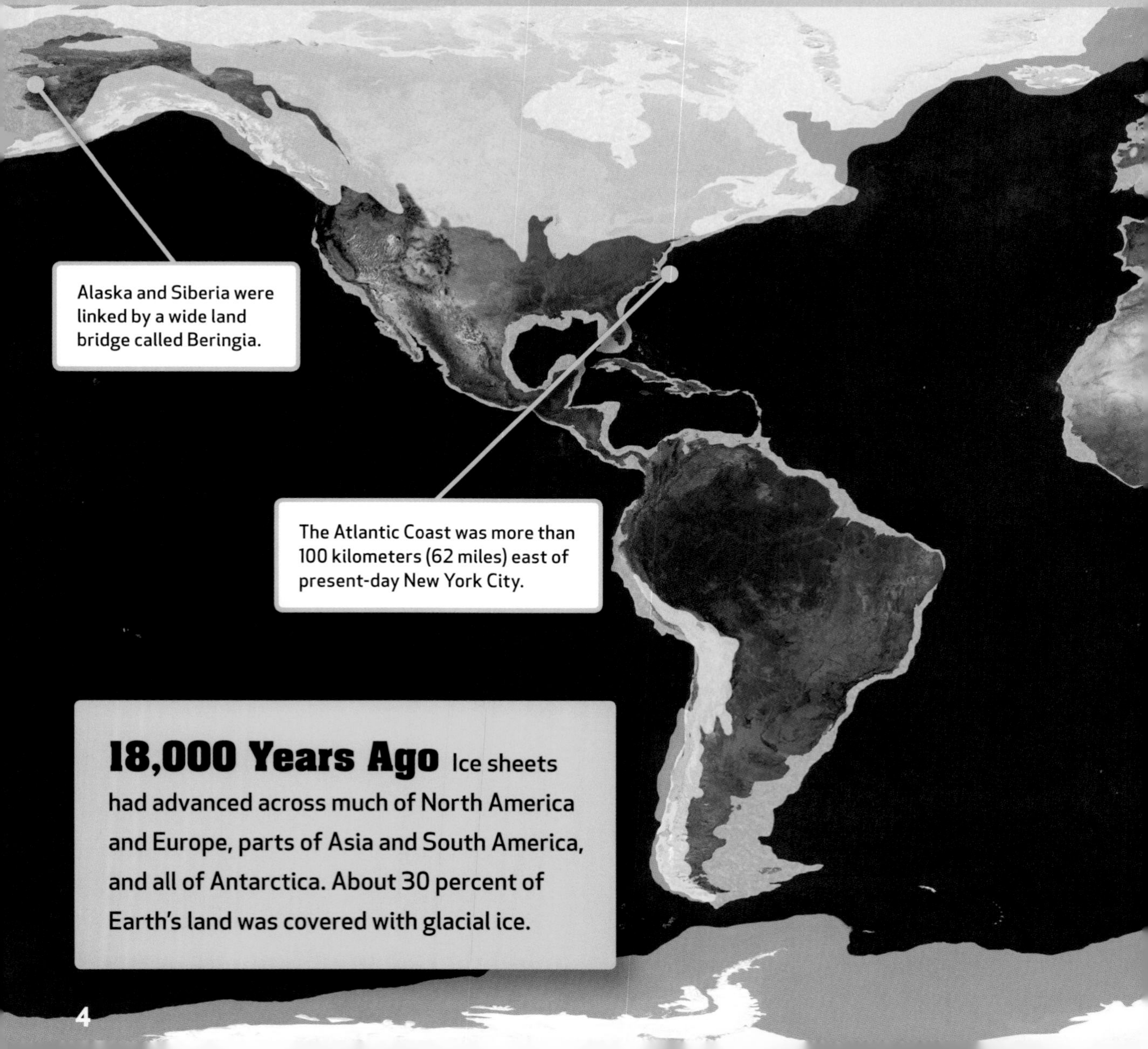

Alaska and Siberia were linked by a wide land bridge called Beringia.

The Atlantic Coast was more than 100 kilometers (62 miles) east of present-day New York City.

18,000 Years Ago Ice sheets had advanced across much of North America and Europe, parts of Asia and South America, and all of Antarctica. About 30 percent of Earth's land was covered with glacial ice.

MORE REAL ESTATE The last ice age also affected Earth's water cycle. Like monster refrigerators, the ice sheets stored more of Earth's water as ice, so the oceans contained less of Earth's water. Sea levels were about 120 meters (394 feet) lower compared with today; there was less ocean and more land. In fact, many places that are now separated by ocean were connected during this time. People could walk from France to Britain, and Siberia was connected to Alaska. People migrated to places where humans had never been before, such as North and South America and Australia.

Today Only about 10 percent of Earth's land is covered with glacial ice.

You could have walked between France and Britain.

Southeast Asia was linked by dry land to the islands of Indonesia.

N
W E
S

Glacial ice
Exposed land

0 3,000 Miles
0 3,000 Kilometers

Turning Up the Heat

The animals and people of the Ice Age were fully adapted to their wintry home. Then about 12,000 years ago, Earth's climate began to warm up. The huge ice sheets shrank and broke apart over a few thousand years. As water from melting ice refilled the oceans, sea levels rose. The rising oceans flooded land bridges, separating groups of people, plants, and animals.

MASS EXTINCTION Many animals that had thrived in the icy tundra went extinct, or died out. Nobody knows exactly why, but scientists have a few theories. Perhaps the animals' food disappeared as the climate changed, or maybe people over-hunted them.

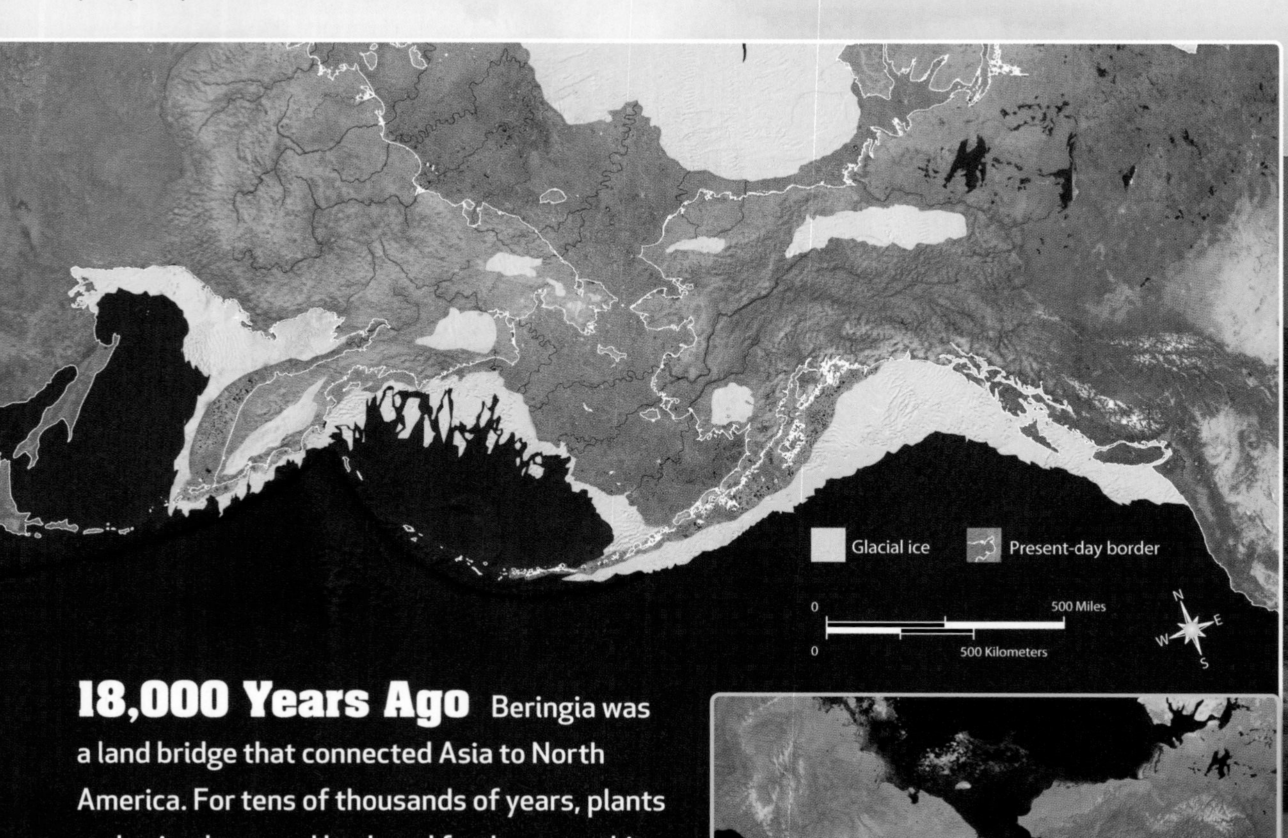

18,000 Years Ago Beringia was a land bridge that connected Asia to North America. For tens of thousands of years, plants and animals spread back and forth across this cold and windy tundra. Humans used Beringia to cross from Asia to North and South America shortly before the seas swallowed it up about 12,500 years ago.

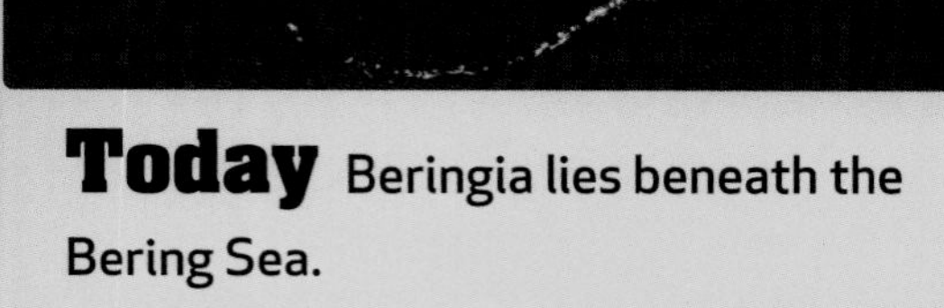

Today Beringia lies beneath the Bering Sea.

A NEW WORLD A new landscape emerged as the ice receded. The moving ice sheets had churned up soil and rock, carrying the rocky debris with them. As the ice sheets shrank, they deposited, or dropped, the rocky material into huge mounds and deep layers. Over time, the mounds became grassy hills, and the layers of sediment became today's fertile farming fields such as those of the Midwestern United States.

The ice sheets also carved new features into the landscape. Jagged V-shaped valleys became smooth, wide, and U-shaped. The rounded hills and broad valleys of England's Lake District, for example, are the work of ice. Some U-shaped valleys were flooded by the rising oceans, forming **fjords.** Fjords can be found around the coasts of Norway, Greenland, Alaska, and other places.

Ice Age glaciers shaped England's Lake District. Glaciers widened the valleys and ground down the hills.

Missoula

FEARSOME FLOODS Although the ice-age meltdown was gradual, it sometimes caused sudden disasters, such as monster floods that swept across North America.

Ice sheets not only plow up land, they can grow huge **glaciers** that branch off. If one of these glaciers crosses a river, it can create an ice dam. That's what happened 15,000 years ago near the border of present-day Idaho and Montana. A glacier that was at least half a mile high and about 37 kilometers (23 miles) wide dammed the Clark Fork River. With nowhere to go, the river water filled the nearby valleys, forming Lake Missoula.

A WALL OF WATER Lake Missoula kept on filling up until it reached into western Montana. It contained more water than Lake Ontario and Lake Erie combined. What do you think happened next? The ice dam burst, releasing a monster wall of water. If you combined all of the rivers on Earth into one river, imagine how much water that one river would contain. Ten times that amount poured out of Lake Missoula.

Glacial Lake Missoula was vast. This is what it might have looked like before the ice dam burst.

The powerful wave thundered west, gouging out miles of rock and forming cliffs and canyons. Underwater whirlpools drilled potholes deep into the bedrock. Several similar floods followed over the next 2,500 years as Lake Missoula kept filling and bursting.

CLIMATE CHANGE The Ice Age glaciers, and the amazing changes they made, remind us that natural climate changes are part of Earth's past. Today's glaciers appear on every continent except Australia. And two vast ice sheets still cover Antarctica and Greenland. These are the remnants of the ice sheets of the last ice age. What will Earth be like thousands of years from now? Judging by the past, we know one thing's for certain: Earth's climate will change.

Lines on the hills around the city of Missoula, Montana, show the different water levels of Lake Missoula. Waves cut into the hills, leaving these lines. The highest one lies 290 meters (950 feet) above the city.

Check In What changes occurred as the planet warmed and the last ice age ended?

GENRE History Article **Read to find out** about the rise and fall of the Greenland Vikings.

Viking Weather

by Stacey Klaman illustrations by Jim Madsen

FROM THE 9TH TO THE 11TH CENTURY, EUROPE'S COASTS AND RIVERS WERE DOMINATED BY **THE VIKINGS.**

The Vikings, or Norse, were farmers and fishermen from Denmark, Norway, and Sweden who craved wealth and adventure. When groups of Norse banded together as warriors, beware! The Vikings were feared for their violent raids on towns. They were also respected as expert traders. From 800–1100 A.D., the Vikings spread out across Europe. They built villages in present-day Russia, England, Ireland, Iceland, and Greenland.

The story of the Greenland Vikings starts with Erik the Red. Erik was reportedly banned from Iceland for murder. So in 982 A.D., he and about 500 other Norse set sail in search of a new island once spoken of by another Viking.

Erik and his Vikings followers had to sail about 280 kilometers (175 miles) west to reach the island. Once there, they sailed into a deep **fjord.** Their timing was perfect. A warmer **climate** had begun sweeping across the Northern Hemisphere only a century earlier. The Vikings found mild weather along the fjord as well as enough open land to support their livestock and crops.

Erik returned to Iceland a few years later to convince other Norse to join him in the new territory he called Greenland. To people living in a place called Iceland, what could sound better than a place called Greenland? In the summer of 986, 24 boatloads of Vikings set sail from Iceland to colonize Greenland. But within 475 years, would climate change defeat the Greenland Vikings?

The Viking settlers unload their longships on Greenland's coast.

Greenland is the world's largest island. About 80 percent of it lies beneath an **ice sheet** about 3.2 kilometers (2 miles) thick. Greenland has a nearly treeless, mountainous coast, and is known for its cold, desert-like conditions. The Vikings arrived on Greenland during a warm period in history. Its ice sheet was slightly smaller, so more coastal land was free of ice.

The Greenland Vikings built two settlements, the first of which was on the southern tip of the island. Archaeologists call this the Eastern Settlement. The Vikings built the smaller Western Settlement along the southwest coast.

Both settlements were located beside fjords, miles from the sea. The fjords protected them from harsh winds and ocean storms. Life was difficult, but the warm climate allowed Vikings to farm as they had in Iceland. Although Iceland is smaller than Greenland, both islands have some similar land features. Greenland's mountains, ice fields, and fjords would've seemed familiar to the newcomers.

The Vikings had built hundreds of farms by 1100. Their cattle, goats, and sheep grazed on pastures year round. Trade

routes were set up across the ice-free seas. The Greenland Vikings imported timber, iron, and tools from Norway and Iceland. They were off to a good start.

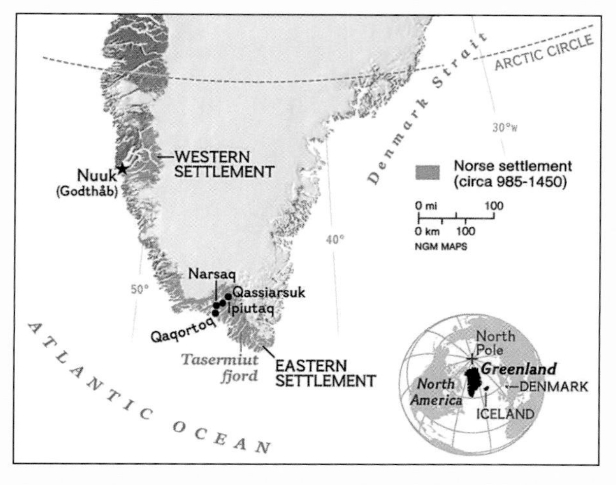

The Vikings founded two colonies. Both were along the grassy coast. Scientists think the Viking population grew to between 4,000 and 5,000 people.

Leif Erikson Sails to America

Erik the Red's son, Leif Erikson, might have been the first European to reach North America from Greenland—500 years before Christopher Columbus. Archaeologists found the remains of an 11th century Viking settlement in Newfoundland, Canada.

Erikson sailed about 2,300 kilometers (1,430 miles) to reach North America. By contrast, Columbus sailed about 6,500 kilometers (4,040 miles) from Spain to the Bahamas.

A warm climate allowed Viking farmers to thrive on Greenland.

Climate seemed an unlikely enemy of the hardy Vikings, but they suffered in a worsening environment. A cooler climate had returned to the Northern Hemisphere by the 14th century. As a result, the seas became stormier, and trade routes from Norway and Iceland became dangerous. Sea ice cut the Greenlanders off from other Norse groups for longer and longer periods each winter. Without fresh supplies from trade ships, living in isolation became more challenging.

Yet the Greenland Vikings were well-adapted to life on the island. The Vikings relied on farming for food and banded together for annual seal hunts in the waters off the coast. But as summers grew shorter and cooler, the Vikings couldn't grow enough hay to feed their livestock through the winter. Even the seals grew scarce as temperatures

These are the ruins of Hvalsey Church. It was the site of a wedding in 1408, the last recorded event in the Norse Greenlander's history.

dropped. The Greenlanders were running out of resources.

Experts think a lack of food may have forced the Vikings to abandon the Western Settlement by the mid-14th century. The Eastern Settlement was abandoned by the early 15th century. After more than four centuries, had the worsening climate conquered the Greenland Vikings?

Hvalsey Church, as it may have looked about 800 years ago.

Greening Again

Greenland is undergoing a shift in climate once again. Today's temperatures are approaching the warmer temperatures of early Viking days, more than a thousand years ago. Greenland and other places near the North and South Poles are warming about twice as fast as most of the world. Right now only about one percent of Greenland can support agriculture. As Greenland's ice sheet keeps shrinking, more land will open up.

Greenland's warming has helped sheep farmers in the southwest of the country. As the growing season lengthens each year, farmers now graze their sheep in pastures year round just like the Vikings used to do.

Warming temperatures are also raising hopes for farmers. They want to grow enough food so that Greenland won't have to import most of its fruits and vegetables anymore. Imported food is costly. Greenland farmers can now grow foods like broccoli and cauliflower, which wasn't possible when temperatures were cooler.

In northern Greenland, however, the warmer temperatures may force a Native American group called the Inuit to change their traditional way of life. The Inuit hunt seals, walruses, and other animals on the vast sea ice for their livelihood. As the sea ice shrinks, animals move to new locations. This makes hunting trips much harder.

Most Greenlanders are descendants of Inuit and of European immigrants who came after the Vikings. With a population of less than 60,000, all Greenlanders will have to adjust. The warming climate will bring about many new opportunities and challenges for everyone.

Greenlander Sten Pedersen picks cabbage only 19 kilometers (12 miles) from the edge of the ice sheet. Warming temperatures have encouraged farmers to try growing new crops, such as cabbage.

A Greenland farmer herds sheep near Qassiarsuk, where Erik the Red raised cattle a thousand years ago.

Check In What can people learn about climate change from the experiences of the Greenland Vikings?

GENRE History Article

Read to find out how art can provide clues to past climate.

Freezing EUROPE

by Stacey Klaman

A picture is worth a thousand words—that's what experts thought while studying the Little Ice Age, a period of Earth's **climate** history that lasted for about 550 years. Along with scientific evidence from ice cores and tree ring growth, researchers studied paintings from this period. Take a look at this painting. What do you see? Snow covers the ground and rooftops under a chilly blue sky. In the distance, people skate on frozen ponds while someone carries kindling across a bridge. It is a winter scene from the distant past.

Hunters in the Snow, 1565

Pieter Bruegel the Elder painted this snapshot of life in the 1560s. The painting depicts one of the first bad winters of the Little Ice Age. Temperatures were just a bit cooler than today's, but this difference had a big impact. European winters became brutally cold. Summers became wetter and shorter, which led to crop failures and famine, or food shortages. Without enough food, Europeans suffered from malnutrition. They were at a greater risk from disease. Skeletons unearthed at burial sites show that the average height of men dropped 6.35 centimeters ($2\frac{1}{2}$ inches) during the 17th and 18th centuries.

Frozen IN TIME

Climate wasn't the only thing to change in the 1500s. Art was also changing. Until then, most artists painted portraits or religious themes. From the 1500s onward, artists painted what they saw around them, too. These scenes from the past show us what life was like during the Little Ice Age, long before photography existed.

***Winter Scene with Ice Skaters*, c. 1608**

A Dutch artist named Hendrick Avercamp painted this winter scene in the Netherlands in the early 1600s. How did the artist portray life during the Little Ice Age? Pale grays and steely blues give the scene its gloomy, wintry feel. A few boats are trapped in the ice, but the people are out and about, using the frozen waterway as a street. Compare the scene with life today. What seems unusual?

Part of Lagoon Which Froze Over in 1708, Venice, Italy

During the winter of 1708–1709, a French duchess is said to have written about the Great Frost, Europe's coldest winter in 500 years. She described it as the most severe winter she had ever lived through. She wasn't exaggerating. Europe became an icy continent as lakes and rivers froze solid. Cattle froze to death in pastures, and sailors died at sea from the cold. Artist Gabriele Bella captured the Great Frost in this painting, which shows the frozen lagoon of Venice, Italy.

The Fair on the Thames, February 4, 1814

During the Little Ice Age, some winters were so cold that the River Thames froze. Whenever this occurred, the people of London would hold a frost fair on the ice. An English army officer described the last frost fair, which was held in 1814. "The people moved across the river by way of what was called Freezeland Street. . . . There were swings, bookstalls, skittle alleys, toyshops, almost everything that might be found in an ordinary fair." This illustration by Luke Clennell shows Londoners enjoying the fair.

What Caused THE LITTLE ICE AGE?

Many scientists think the Little Ice Age had multiple causes. They think it was the result of a "perfect storm" of events involving volcanoes, sea ice, and ocean currents.

Volcanoes Scientists think a 50-year period of massive volcanic eruptions released a huge amount of volcanic **aerosols,** or sun-blocking particles, into the atmosphere. The aerosols would have prevented some of the sun's energy from reaching Earth's surface, resulting in a cooler planet. The temperature difference could have started a chain of events beginning with sea ice.

Sea ice The amount of Arctic sea ice increased and drifted south along the coast of Greenland. When it reached the warmer waters of the North Atlantic, the sea ice melted.

Sea ice is frozen fresh water. Fresh water is less dense, or lighter, than salt water, so when the sea ice melted, the fresh water would have stayed at the surface. The entire North Atlantic could have been covered with a layer of cold fresh water. The layer may have disrupted ocean currents.

Ocean currents Ocean currents move water around the planet. Cold waters move south as warm waters move north. The ocean's temperature affects the surrounding air temperature. That's why living near a current of warm water will result in milder winters, such as those experienced in northern Europe. So the ocean currents must have changed to make Europe cooler.

Scientists think volcanic eruptions in Iceland might have triggered the Little Ice Age. In this illustration, the Swedish artist Olaus Magnus (1490–1558) pictures several Icelandic eruptions. What does the artist believe caused them? What does it show you about people's ideas about volcanoes in the early 1500s?

Mount Pinatubo is a volcano in the Philippines. When it erupted in 1991, it shot millions of tons of ash and gas 34 kilometers (22 miles) into the air. Ash and gas circled the globe. As a result, Earth's temperature dropped by about 0.5°C (1°F) for the next two years.

The cold fresh water from melted sea ice changed the ocean currents. Less warm water now flowed north toward Europe. The colder ocean temperatures changed the climate. Europeans began experiencing cooler summers and colder winters. The cooler temperatures produced even more Arctic sea ice. The cycle continued for centuries!

The Little Ice Age had a big effect on northern and central Europe. Whatever might have caused the Little Ice Age, evidence of its impact is found in surprising places, from skeletal remains to famous works of art.

Check In What do scientists think caused the Little Ice Age?

GENRE Science Article | Read to find out how Earth's climate is changing.

Climate Ch

by Robert Phalen

The year is 2384 A.D. The United States flag outside your school has forty-six stars instead of fifty. Your history book mentions drowned countries, and sunken cities such as London, Berlin, Rome, Sydney, Buenos Aires, Beijing, and Tokyo. Their names are familiar to you, but easily forgotten. After all, now these places are just underwater ruins full of fish.

Your history book also mentions New York City, Boston, Los Angeles, San Francisco, Seattle, Houston, and other cities that were in the United States. None of them exist now, but some of your ancestors came from those places. In your book, you read that there was once a state jutting out of the East Coast. It was part of something called the Gulf of Mexico.

Could Earth change this much in just a few hundred years? **Climate** change is happening now, and rising seas are just the tip of the iceberg. (Icebergs don't exist in 2384.) What's the forecast for the next few centuries, and how will people adapt?

nundrum

Divers explore the ruins of an ancient temple off the coast of Alexandria, Egypt. The temple used to overlook the lost city of Herakleion. Rising sea levels, earthquakes, and tsunamis sank the city more than a thousand years ago. Parts of nearby Alexandria suffered a similar fate.

In the Heat of the Moment

Climate change has happened many times before. The planet has been both warmer and cooler than it is now. Past climate changes were triggered by natural causes such as volcanic eruptions and small changes in Earth's orbit.

Stepping on the Gas Most climate scientists agree that much of today's climate change is caused by human activities. We're adding a large amount of **greenhouse** gases to the air by burning fossil fuels. Greenhouse gases are part of Earth's atmosphere. They produce the greenhouse effect, which keeps our planet comfy. Without greenhouse gases, Earth would be too cold for life as we know it to exist.

But too much greenhouse gas in the atmosphere traps too much heat and raises the global temperature. It's called **global warming,** and it's happening right now. Even if we stopped using fossil fuels tomorrow, Earth would continue to heat up.

A supercell thunderstorm near Medicine Lodge, Kansas, produced baseball-sized hail. Severe weather will happen more often as the planet heats up.

It's the Future, to a Degree

Would you guess the Rocky Mountains affect the climate in Norway? The mountains steer air masses southward, where they absorb heat and moisture before heading to Norway. Without the Rockies, Norway would be 5–10°C (9–18°F) cooler. Earth's climate involves millions of these interactions. That's why predicting future climate is difficult and never exact.

Climate scientists use giant supercomputers to help them make predictions. These machines make more than a quadrillion calculations per second (1 quadrillion = 1,000,000,000,000,000). In 2012, engineers built a supercomputer called Yellowstone, which will help scientists make more accurate climate models. The latest climate predictions show a temperature rise of 1.4–5.6°C (2.5–10°F) over the next 100 years.

An engineer installs part of the Yellowstone supercomputer, located in Cheyenne, Wyoming. Imagine if you counted every grain of sand on every beach in the world. That's how many calculations it can do in one hour!

More Surf, Less Turf

Rising air temperatures bring rising sea levels. Since 1880, global sea levels have risen by about 20 centimeters (8 inches). As the seas creep higher, more land gets swallowed up. By the time you are old enough to retire, the ocean could be as much as 1 meter (3 feet) above present level. If that happened, low-lying cities like Miami and New Orleans would have to be abandoned.

What's causing sea levels to rise? It's not the melting of ice floating in the sea. No, the real culprit is ice on land. Melting **glaciers** and **ice sheets** are adding more water to the ocean.

Most land ice is locked in the ice sheets on Greenland and Antarctica. These huge slabs of ice hold more than 99 percent of Earth's fresh water. Both ice sheets, however, are getting smaller. If Greenland's ice sheet melted completely, it would cause sea levels to rise by about 6 meters (20 feet). What if both ice sheets melted? Scientists think the ocean would rise by 70 meters (230 feet)! Luckily a complete meltdown won't happen any time soon.

Even so, a little sea rise can cause big problems. Almost half of the world's population lives near the ocean. Salty seawater can destroy habitats and contaminate drinking water. Higher sea levels mean powerful waves will cause major flooding in low-lying areas. Is there an upside to all of this doom and gloom? It depends on where you live. Landlocked towns could have great ocean views in a few hundred years.

Ocean Commotion Global warming is also making ocean water warmer. Warmer waters threaten coral reefs, which are in danger.

Rapidly melting sea ice is a threat to many polar animals. Sea ice provides emperor penguins, seals, and polar bears with a place to hunt, breed, and feed. The survival of polar animals will depend on how well they adjust to increasing temperatures and decreasing ice.

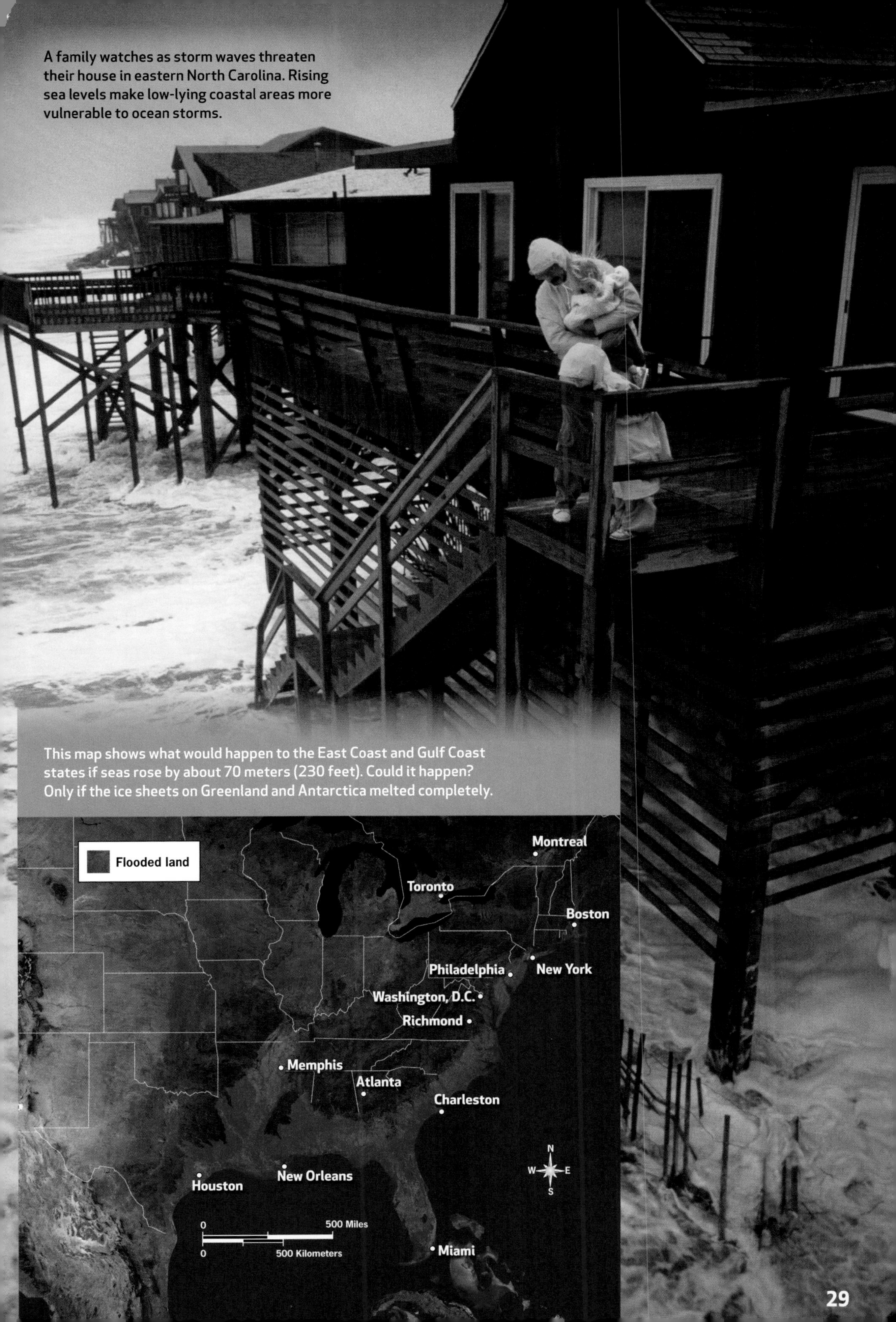

A family watches as storm waves threaten their house in eastern North Carolina. Rising sea levels make low-lying coastal areas more vulnerable to ocean storms.

This map shows what would happen to the East Coast and Gulf Coast states if seas rose by about 70 meters (230 feet). Could it happen? Only if the ice sheets on Greenland and Antarctica melted completely.

Earth 2.0

What will happen if global warming continues unchecked? Memphis is currently about 1,160 kilometers (720 miles) from the coast. Fast-forward to 2384. The land might be so different that a billboard reads, "Come see the sea in Memphis, Tennessee!" How else might Earth be different by 2384, or sooner?

On the Move Unchecked global warming will reshuffle life around the planet. Plant and animal populations will constantly have to migrate to keep up with shifting climates. Many species won't be able to adapt to hotter, dryer, or wetter environments. For example, polar bears, penguins, and redwood forests may become extinct. They will seem as strange to the people of 2384 as woolly mammoths seem to us today. Thankfully, many of Earth's animals and plants will survive climate change, and some may even thrive.

Humans will have to migrate, too. The number of "climate refugees" will skyrocket, and people living in less hard-hit regions will need to share their resources.

Wild Weather Hurricanes, tornadoes, and other forms of wild weather will be much more common. The planet is already experiencing more extreme weather. If global warming keeps up, the weather will just get weirder. Climate scientists predict wetter springs and falls, and dryer summers and winters in the U.S. The southwest United States will get dryer and even hotter. By 2384, it could be a scorching desert. Water shortages would force most people living there to relocate.

Crop Flop Extreme wet and dry weather will be hard on crops. Droughts, insects, and plant diseases could cause widespread famines, or food shortages. On the other hand, plants will have a longer growing season. People may have to grow new kinds of crops that can survive these hazards.

Climate change is nothing new, but human activities are now contributing to it. The pace of climate change is faster than usual, too. Climate scientists are still struggling to understand its effects. In the meantime, the future is undecided.

As habitats melt away, polar bears go hungry for longer periods of time.

If humans can help slow the pace of global warming, the effects of climate change will be much less severe in years to come.

Check In How might climate change affect you during your lifetime?

Discuss

1. What connections can you make between the four pieces in *Earth's Crazy Climate*? How are the pieces related?

2. Use specific information in "When the Ice Melted" to explain how the last ice age affected Earth's water cycle.

3. How do you think Greenland's climate may have "defeated" the Greenland Vikings?

4. Compare and contrast the causes and effects of climate changes in "Freezing Europe" and "Climate Conundrum." What do they reveal about the link between weather and climate?

5. What do you still wonder about Earth's crazy climate? What would be some good ways to find more information?